To everyone who desires to be
rich and prosperous.

BE RICH!

Thoughts and Principles to create wealth

Simone Pitchon

authorHOUSE®

AuthorHouse™ UK Ltd.
500 Avebury Boulevard
Central Milton Keynes, MK9 2BE
www.authorhouse.co.uk
Phone: 08001974150

Published by AuthorHouse 12/30/2011

ISBN: 978-1-4670-0848-8 (sc)
ISBN: 978-1-4670-0849-5 (e)

Preface

The conductor line of this book is a simple principle, but which is very difficult to work on in our minds. It is called: Prosperous Thought or Rich Thought. Most human beings want to be rich, prosperous, successful and, definitely, we should be, this is the human evolution. However how many of us keep constantly in our minds the thought of being rich? I emphasise, keep constantly the thought of wealth and abundance in our mind. Have this ideal as your aim in life.

Wealth is a state of mind. First, it starts in our way of thinking and acting and interacting with the Universe. The real wealth is inside. We should begin to be rich by our ideas and thoughts. We need to be always guided by great and successful thoughts. Consequently, when we remove the thoughts of failure and defeat from our brain, prosperity begins to be part of our lives.

Everyone who reads, understands and applies this philosophy is well prepared to attract a magic life and enjoy the most sublime states that are denied and blocked for most of us.

This philosophy of being rich and creating wealth is a machine that needs to be engaged. Wealth is intertwined with the way we work our mental world and how we act in the physical world.

The Universe is large and prosperous, nature is rich and abundant, and it does not save and does not economise. It blows opulence. We are part of this prosperity and abundance, our lives were planned to be rich and powerful. The power of being rich is within us, we all have the same ability to get the things we want from life.

The multi millionaires in the world do not have a different brain from people who are starving and are not better than them; they simply know how to enable the power that is within their minds. The only thing that differs one median person from a millionaire is the power of thoughts, their ardent desire and the conviction that they can win and they can make things happen.

There is no limit to creations, projects and amount of money that we may have. You can not have wealth unless you want to work in a powerful way with a passionate desire for money and really believe that you will have great wealth.

If you have little money today it is because your thoughts are limited and you feel bad more than you feel good regarding the life you have, or you are focusing your energy thinking about other things that are not prosperity and welfare. So what are you thinking now? How do you feel now? Start to channel the power of your thoughts and feelings to wealth immediately, wherever you go and whoever you are with. Do not divert yourself with other negative thoughts. Bring success into your life!

Introduction

It is nothing new that the economic problems are one of those major issues that affect all countries and people around the world. As I was born in Brazil, I did not escape this dilemma. I lived with this problem for a long time in my life because I am the daughter of a middle class family that always had great difficulty in paying accounts and debts, like most other Brazilian families.

Brazil is a very rich country, but has big problems in its distribution of wealth and income for its people; unfortunately many Brazilians still are hungry in a country that produces so much food.

I was always concerned with my lack of money and the limitations of other Brazilian citizens, as well as the enormous wealth possessed by a rich minority. It is a great contrast to those who live in this land. So I started looking for a solution to this issue. I began to study about the life of the great millionaires and successful people on the planet.

At the beginning of my previous book "What we want, we get it! - Improvement of the ideas and thoughts" I explained that the essence of wealth is a seed of positive thought that should always be watered. If you have prosperity in your mind, sooner or later it will appear in your pocket.

If you want to be rich, think rich. Do not think of the lack of money just think about money. Do not think about bills and debts, think of the checks you will receive.

I state again that thought produces things, and your thoughts, when tuned to money and wealth, will lead you to money and wealth. If your thoughts are tuned to prosperity the result will be prosperity. Thinking rooted in poverty and difficulty will result in the increase of poverty and difficulty.

It is with great affection that I introduce this book to you which is a collection of good thoughts to attract wealth and prosperity. My intention is that you read it every day, not necessarily in the same order, and keep in your mind a continuous abundance of rich thoughts and good feelings. After some time you will no longer need this tool because it will be all in your mind automatically and hopefully your purpose will be achieved.

The task is within yourself; you must shake off negative thoughts and feelings and change them as soon as possible. This is the key to your prosperous life. I hope you have the wisdom and strength inside you to walk into the path of success, wealth and personal ascension.

Simple Ways for Assuring Success

I realise that the correct use of my mind opens the door to a happy, healthy, and wealthy life. It makes my dreams come true. Man transforms his world to richness through his thoughts, emotions, words and actions.

if you ask me, to live and not be rich is a missed opportunity, because we have all the tools inside us to be as wealthy as we can be. Sometimes we feel guilty about wanting to be prosperous, which is totally wrong. Otherwise prosperity should be considered a spiritual blessing. As a child of God we must be wealthy and prosperous in this journey. We deserve to be rich, we were born to be. Ask God for guidance about all your affairs and financial issues and you will be surprised how much better your life will change. God is the creator of this entire rich Universe. He isn't poor and He is such a lovely Father. God works in our favour in every situation; He is our source of wealth.

Our mind is the connecting link with the richness and prosperity that is the power of prosperous thinking. What we radiate through our thoughts, feelings, mental pictures and words we attract into our lives. We must radiate in order to attract. We always have more to give than we realise. We can give light, warm words, and positive thoughts. All things can be accomplished within the mind first; our mind is the divine source for everything we want to achieve. Mentally radiate what you wish to experience in life. The more you tune your mind to rich directions, the less poor you feel.

We are a magnet with the power to attract to ourselves everything that we desire, according to our thoughts, feelings, and mental pictures. We are the centre of our Universe. We attract what we choose to have, good or bad conditions. But from this moment on I choose health, success and wealth. This is a rich Universe and I accept, with all my heart, its richness!

Do whatever you can to feel rich, to feel the rich atmosphere, the rich look. Never think of yourself as poor or needy. Begin thinking in terms of prosperity, and you will find it in abundance that is everywhere. Invite complete prosperity and success to your life now. Desire the highest and the best in your life. There is no reason to feel guilty to ask God what you really desire. List the things you want and dare to declare it to yourself every day. Some desires can be achieved in about six months just as some of mine have been. Others can be achieved in two years. I ardently use this powerful affirmation "I am the child of a loving Father and I have the right to have all my dreams come true."

Mornings are a good start to visualise your new and abundant life. I always start by making a prayer to God. Give thanks for everything (which is absolutely important). Give thanks for your clothing, meals, beauty, home, family, love and friends. Sit down for a few minutes invoking the creative law of prosperity.

I start my day imagining: "This, or something better, now manifests for me in totally satisfying and harmonious ways, for the highest good of all concerned." If you believe it, you'll see it. Every single cell in your body is affected by every single thought you have. You get everything you want if you know how to feel it into being.

The more we focus on what we don't have, the greater our negative energies will grow. Whatever we're feeling is what we're vibrating, and whatever we're vibrating is what we're attracting. If what you are saying or thinking makes you feel like going to the heavens, then you are in the right path.

At nights I usually stop thinking about troubles during my day and stop putting anything negative into my mind. When facing any adverse issue write down how you wish your life might be. Make lists regarding the life you wish to have. Your mind will work to serve you. What is it you ardently desire most in your life? Be definite, clear and sincere about it. Man can create anything he can imagine. Remember, success is created mentally first.

One of my financial desires was to be free to shop anytime, so I spent my minutes imagining a high standard of living. I didn't feel discouraged and didn't give up hope. I was making my fortune imagining it!

Change your mental images and thinking, change your talk, and stop having negative conversations with people. Be careful about what you say. You command through words. Speak only when you have something good to say. Create your new and prosperous life saying nice words. Declare and affirm the good you want for your life. Declare over and over again. At least three minutes a day. Command what you wish by positive statements.

Give others your rich thoughts by thinking of them as rich, successful and prosperous. It is a great way to help them. Anything you say or meditate to help others is worth the effort. In other circumstances visualise people in a good mood when they are angry. View the people passing by on the streets with love. Affirm: "I love all people and all people love me. I live in harmony in this world." Generate and radiate love for others, for yourself and all mankind. As you express love, it comes back to you multiplied. Love is the most important thing to be giving, regardless of the circumstances.

Discipline yourself, save your energy and time, associate only with other prosperous-minded people, with whom you have compatible interests. You should discard failure-prone people. Read prosperous books, conserve prosperous thinking.

There is nothing to fear, divine results are coming for you. Everyone and everything works for you. Overcome fear of any sort. Say no to unhappy experiences. When suffering comes, calm yourself and centre your attention on God. Prayers are the secret to re-gain peace.

To have a better and harmonious life I increase the attention that I give to what is positive and uplifting, and in this way you will radically change the way you feel. It means that we direct our thoughts rather than being directed by them. You are not delegating your life; you are creating your life. You have the power to create. Your power is so strong that whatever you believe comes true. Your whole reality, everything you believe, is your creation. Within you right now there is the power to do things you never dreamed possible.

This power becomes available to you just as soon as you can change your beliefs. There is no action in the entire Universe that is more delicious than inspired action.

If you believe yourself to be beautiful, you become so. If you believe yourself to be rich you will get it by the same principle, you just need to act upon your inspired ideas and make daily steps in the direction of your dreams. You can only become what you dare to imagine.

You deserve it all. You deserve to have all of your aspirations realised. To have it all you must learn to identify a good feeling from a bad feeling. Learn the simple steps of manipulating your feelings and a whole new world of plenty opens up for you. The more emotion you charge your thoughts with, the clearer the picture turns out to be. We get what we emotionally focus on.

We came here, to this blessed planet, and some of our goals are to find ways to feel good most of the time, not just some of the time. As we think, we feel; as we feel, we vibrate; as we vibrate, we attract all the nice things we want to our lives. What has been in our life comes directly from where our focus has been. Negative vibrations occur when we refuse to allow ourselves to think about what makes us happy.

Be a person you would like to listen to: encouraging, tolerant, curious, warm, interesting, and positive. It is possible. Your own life experience is the greatest teacher you will ever have. Pay attention, with all your senses. Today is a new beginning for you to start being a new person. The Creator of the Universe helps us to become Masters of gratitude, generosity, and love, so that we can enjoy all of your creations forever and ever. Progress is impossible without change, and those who can not change their minds can not change anything. Remember the importance of gratitude and appreciation in all areas of your life.

Make time each day to connect with God and with yourself. Give yourself the time and quiet space to be alone with the invisible you. Miracles are waiting for you in that spectacular space.

Remind yourself: I can think differently and my moods and feelings will follow. When you feel prosperous, only things that feel like prosperity can come to you. The more I feel good, the more I attract my desires.

Ask yourself when a crisis erupts, what do I have to learn from this experience right now? I know there's a gift hidden for me in this misfortune, and I'll focus on looking for it. Keep your life focused on believing in yourself and all that you are capable of.

The first principle of success is desire, knowing what you want. Whatever you are searching for and desiring, it is itself also searching for and desiring you. Have faith and take appropriate actions of thoughts, feelings and behaviours towards it.

Believe that you will make your life better. Get away from the unpleasant feelings. Open your mind to the good thoughts and things which lead yourself to positive creating. It is very important we understand what it is that gives joy and passion to our lives and makes life worth living. What do you want? What do you truly want? Let your imagination run and search it. Dream the dream of joy, pleasure, excitement, always dream. The universe gives us what we are feeling every day. My intention is to find joy throughout the day. And I always get it!

Dare to dream new dreams, put your old negative thinking far from you and let it to go away. Give yourself permission to want. There is only one way to stop the mess in our lives from getting worse - stop focusing on them.

Change your focus to something more pleasant so you can change your energy. Find something to feel good about now! Get away from unpleasant feelings, get into pleasant desires. Focus away from the negative vibration and focus on feel good vibes. No circumstances are beyond our control. With our attention on what we joyfully want in life, the desirable things come to us. Try to be in high frequency all the time.

Turn yourself on some kind of happiness. Our goal is to take our focus off our anxiety or grief, and find the feeling of bliss. Have thoughts beyond the things you don't like and focus on what you do like. Change your attention to something more pleasant so you can change your energy.

When you get really angry or upset find something else to think about, stay there, quiet, until your feelings change, then you can be sure that your energy also changes, the longer you stay good, the quicker good things will start to happen.

Find anything to feel good about, do whatever it takes. It is how you flow your energy that makes amazing actions into your life. Step away from bad vibrations. Dive into the wonderful feelings of how fantastic it will be when you get there.

The vibe of appreciation is the most important; it is close to the love that expands throughout the cosmos: If we appreciate anyone or anything all the time our life will be like heaven. Flow the appreciation for your life now; be in love and you will feel yourself alive.

When we feel good or happy we are inviting good experiences. If you want to change something, you have to change the way you think about it. Say yes to a good life, agree with well-being, happiness, richness, loveliness, and everything will be all right.

I don't want to sacrifice my life and dreams for negative feelings. Allow yourself the joy of bathing in a fantasy at least for 15 minutes a day and be enchanted with the life you want to have.

Now I introduce to you some of my rich thoughts and actions I conceived during my studies in order to reach a prosperous, wealthy and happy life. These lines will help you to improve your way of thinking, feeling, and the way of living for your spiritual development in this world:

1.

I focus on the wealth and prosperity in my life. The thought of affluence is constantly in my mind. I have continuously creative and rich thoughts. As a result, I continually attract positive circumstances and richness.

2.

The Law of Attraction is always working in my favour. I attract what I think. I keep a positive vibration and I get lots of money.

3.

With my thoughts I can have what I want and need.

4.

I have a clear understanding of my gifts, talents and interests and use them to achieve what I desire.

5.

I create my own opportunities.

6.

I have the habit of thinking based on the principles of success.

7.

Make use of repetition: "I can do it, I am a winner, I am already very rich". This training brings fortune for many people.

8.

I live my life with enthusiasm, passion and great abundance.

9.

My wealth begins in my mental world. I mentalize richness and sublime things. I have no time for bad thoughts and meanness.

10.

From my thoughts of wealth and abundance I become rich day by day.

11.

Think about how and where you would spend your bunch of cash.

12.

Make a list of things you would buy with the money you will have.

13.

Think about how you would help people with the money you will receive.

14.

Declare every day that you always attract money.

15.

Feel good. Laugh a lot. Stay close to positive and clever people. This feeling helps you to become more prosperous.

16.

**Say every day that you
have loads of money.**

17.

Have a precise value of the amount of money you want.

18.

Be sure that money is coming to you!

19.

Do not doubt that you will be rich.

20.

Stop and think: Are you bringing money close to you or pushing money away from you by your own thoughts?

21.

Be grateful for the money you already have.

22.

Do not think about how you can win money, this is the task of the Universe which interacts with your thoughts and makes your wish come true. Just think about how much you want to win.

23.

Give money to those who have less than you.

24.

Be happy now! Do not put obstacles in your life as: "Just when I have this or that I will be happy." Do whatever you can to feel joyful and plenty today.

25.

Do not talk about lack of money at any time of your life.

26.

It only depends on you to attract or repel money by your power of thinking. Do not think about your debts. Do not stress because of them. Think of your wallet full of money.

27.

Do not get anxious because you have little money. Appreciate the money you have today.

28.

You have to be grateful for the little from today to be able to get much more from tomorrow.

29.

Appreciate rich people around you and all the beautiful things they built with their money.

30.

Do not feel jealous of someone who has more money than you.

31.

Think you are getting rich now.

32.

Fall in love with money and welfare.

33.

Open your wallet and enjoy the money you have in it. Touch it. Give thanks for the amount you already have.

34.

Repeat constantly: Money comes to me easily.

35.

**You have value to the world
and this is the reason why you
should always get some more.**

36.

Add in your paper money some zeros so that it turns to millions. Look at it every day.

37.

Know that you are perfect and you deserve all the wealth of the universe.

38.

Take your attention away from things that do not make you feel well such as debts, bills and creditors.

39.

Your main goal is a lot of money. Forget all the rest that brings you down.

40.

You by your own are who manages your cash.

41.

No one is guilty for your lack of money, only you and your limited thoughts.

42.

It does not matter how much you earn in your job now, give thanks for it.

43.

You can get the amount you wrote on your paper money if you trust in the power of your thought and nice feelings.

44.

**Do not blame or criticise
your current situation.**

45.

Whatever your financial situation is now, it can be changed by your positive mind.

46.

Visualise the income you want.

47.

Image yourself in your dream job.

48.

Think. Think a lot about the exact value of the salary you want.

49.

Read about the wealth of others and fortune in general.

50.

Research about prosperity, read articles about wealth and welfare. Explore the sources of knowledge.

51.

Everything that you believe to be yours, you will reach. Have faith.

52.

Believe that this philosophy is able to bring material wealth for you. Many have used it.

53.

Thinking about success and wealth is a politic against defeat.

54.

Mentalize your life: Abundant, powerful, the way you have been always dreaming about.

55.

Wish. Wish so much to be very rich. M-U-C-H, really!

56.

Thoughts, ideas and organised plans are everything that a person needs to succeed. Be determined to be rich.

57.

The wealth is not just material. It begins with a good and helpful spirit.

58.

The spirit of wealth is based on donation and altruism. Help others always!

59.

Do not be selfish. Think about the welfare of others, so you provide and create your own welfare.

60.

Stop to think and reflect. This is an exercise. You have to sit down in a calm atmosphere and focus on thinking rich, often.

61.

As an athlete exercises his muscles running, swimming, etc. you should exercise your brain thinking about success, abundance and wealth. It is not as easy as it sounds, but with practice it becomes automatic.

62.

You win and become a successful person by the determination and firm purpose, persistence and strong desire of getting rich.

63.

The desire impulses your thoughts. Thought is the creative formula of all richness.

64.

A determined man bets his entire future on his desire. Stake your life in the art of being rich. This is the secret.

65.

Never give up on your dream until it materialises.

66.

The intangible transforms into the tangible by the power of feelings, so feel rich and you will have wealth.

67.

The time to acquire wealth is proportional to your willingness and determination plus the force of your thoughts.

68.

Disregard all the contrary attitudes to get wealth and fortune as well as greed and meanness.

69.

**Initiative, faith and
willpower are the basic
forces to achieve wealth.**

70.

Do not quit when difficulties come up.

71.

Rich is a person who persists.

72.

Your ardent desire is transmuted into gold.

73.

When defeat or failure happens the majority of people give up. Change this scenario.

74.

It is the power of thought that enables an ignorant. You do not need to have a PhD to become rich.

75.

The answer to success will come to your mind when you control the secrets of the Universal Law that says: Everything comes from your mind and from the power of thinking about prosperity.

76.

When you believe in your mental power, your financial status changes and everything that you touch begins to grow and improve.

77.

Be aware that you are a success. This is very important!

78.

You may not think in terms of poverty, misery, failure and defeat if you really want to be rich.

79.

Everything comes to your benefit when you are acting in accordance with the Universal Law and the principles of support, kindness and gratitude.

80.

Make your desire for wealth greater and more powerful than your weakness and sadness.

81.

Our power within operates on both sides: to bring us prosperity and welfare and also to bring scarcity and poverty.

82.

Dynamic and productive thinking makes us rich. Weak and impotent thinking make us powerless and poor.

83.

No matter how your situation is now, work on your belief. You can do it. You can achieve! Yes you can.

84.

Your defined desire for fortune transcends and goes beyond any barrier. Stake your future on being rich.

85.

**Say every day: I'm rich.
The power of affirmation
is very strong.**

86.

The difference between the fortunate ones and those who fail is in perseverance, do not change the path for the easiest way or quit in the middle of the road, maintain your purpose.

87.

Keep in your mind the certain amount of money you want. It is not enough talking about: "I want a lot of money". Have the clear value in your head. Visualize this amount.

88.

Determine the amount that you will give in return for the money you will receive. This is fundamental.

89.

Wealthy people are usually happy. A good sense of humour is very important.

90.

Create a plan to fulfil your desire and begin at once.

91.

Stop for five minutes and feel how it is good to be wealthy. What would money bring to you: Security? Peace? Comfort? Happiness? Good health? Spend some of your time on those pleasant feelings.

92.

Read your positive statements. View clearly your dreams getting closer to you as a daydreamer. Feel happy and passionate. Believe in the possession of your money.

93.

Only those who become aware of their fortune can accumulate great wealth.

94.

Those that accumulate great riches first had big dreams, high hopes and added value in the lives of others before getting a lot of money.

95.

Every powerful man was or is as big a dreamer as Walt Disney.

96.

If you do not see your beautiful fortune in your imagination, you never see money in your bank account.

97.

Live a life of service to others.

98.

Focus on your personal dreams, goals and desires.

99.

Continuously I have positive thoughts; continuously I attract positive circumstances into my life.

100.

I live my life with passion, intelligence and inner truth.

101.

Desire. Desire a lot to be rich.

102.

All those who were rich in this world were reasonable to give and be altruistic.

103.

Keep trying no matter how difficult the situation is.

104.

Failure comes to those who allow it.

105.

The more you give, the more you achieve!

106.

**The greatest happiness
and success comes
from being in love.**

107.

Dreamers never give up.

108.

The world is full of "many" or "money" opportunities.

109.

Do not be depressed by failure. Do not accept defeat.

110.

There is no 'impossible' for those who desire ardently.

111.

Have faith in yourself!

112.

Believe in the miracles of God.

113.

Write down on paper – "I am getting richer everyday". It is a great tool to work with your subconscious mind.

114.

Concentrate at least 15 minutes a day on your purpose; create a clear image of your richness.

115.

No richness can last if it is not built on truth, justice and love.

116.

Negative attitudes towards other people will never bring your success.

117.

The power of faith is enormous. Take Gandhi as an example and his power of believing in himself.

118.

**Poverty and welfare can not
be in the same thought.**

119.

Have control of your environment and you will control your rich thoughts.

120.

Which TV Programs and movies do you watch? Which music do you listen to? Which books do you read? Who are the people you talk to? Feed your mind with thoughts of creative things.

121.

Close your eyes and concentrate on your money.

122.

The Universal Mind will inspire you to achieve your goal.

123.

Use the right positive affirmations and meditate on your purpose of getting rich. Use your imagination.

124.

At night forget all your problems and concentrate on the exact amount of money you want and the amount of money you will give to others in return.

125.

Your thought of being rich is the same thought that nature created Earth with and all the substances from the Universe.

126.

Wake up with your feelings of being rich.

127.

The money comes as a result from one idea, a desire nourished by your mind.

128.

When your plan fails, it is just for a moment. Re-start again! Thomas Edison was unsuccessful so many times and never gave up. In fact he was not a failure. Those were steps for his success.

129.

**You can not be open to
receive all your prosperity
and welfare if you are holding
onto resentment or revenge.**

130.

Your health and wealth will start improving dramatically on the day you forgive.

131.

If you can not forgive someone you can not be open to abundance.

132.

If you are holding onto revenge let love walk into your life.

133.

No matter how bad you think you are, you have a Creator who had already forgiven you.

134.

You must forgive yourself first, so a life of prosperity can shine for you.

135.

Forgive everyone with whom you are out of harmony.

136.

Ask for forgiveness from the people you have wronged in the past.

137.

One of the greatest barriers to freedom from debt is fear and desperation. When they are overcome, you are on your way to financial freedom.

138.

When you are in perfect harmony with your inner world and greet every day with the most profound gratitude, everything else is just a matter of time.

Important Steps

A. Summarizing the rich way of life:

1. Give thanks to God during your day, whenever you remember.
2. Write down your desires and rich dreams on paper.
3. Imagine your wealthy life coming to you.
4. Affirm the rich thoughts in this book as often as you can.
5. Feel good, no matter what. Feeling good attracts your prosperous life.

B. My advice for you is to plan a week of love. In the following week, feel wonder about everything and everyone. Be grateful, feel excited and enthusiastic, feel the power of God in your life, feel how amazing it is to be alive. Change your vibrations about doing things which give you pleasure. The better you feel inside, the better your life will be!

C. Choose one day of the week to pray for people you love, family and friends or those who are facing problems, or even people from another country who need help. By the power of love contained in your statements you can heal, you can help, you can transform lives! It is miraculous.

D. Love yourself, love others, forgive and move ahead.

These methods will fill you with inner knowing, and also make you become more confident and stronger. Consequently it will eliminate trouble from your mind and guide you into the greatest experience about controlling your life; you are now a prosperous thinker!

Final Words

I am a big dreamer... I have a great imagination and great faith in God and in myself. I am more than happy to share these lines with you, because this is my life experience. I have got a plentiful life through this method. Today I am an extremely grateful person for everything that I have reached and achieved through my positive thoughts and wonderful feelings. I always think about a positive and cheerful way to live this magical life.

Life is very beautiful and important. It is not worth going through it in a bad mood and with tons of concerns. Try using the thought of prosperity and rich thinking to be a high spirited person. Wealth begins inside, in your mind, in your soul. Then it turns into physical objects. To achieve wealth, think of wealth and abundance. Donate, donate much. Give thanks for everything you already have and smile!

Wishing you happiness and prosperity! Lots of love,

Simone Pitchon.